A Royal Romance

Trevor Hall

COLOUR LIBRARY BOOKS

Programme

This familiar panorama of the city of Westminster has provided the setting for almost every major royal wedding this century. From Buckingham Palace (top left) long processions of royal carriages have set off down the famous red expanse of the Mall towards the two component parts of Nash's graceful Carlton House Terrace. Between them stands the Duke of York's column, at which point processions have headed right into Horse Guards (top right), across the Parade and through the Arch into Whitehall. Another right turn leads down Whitehall, past a succession of government buildings, to Parliament Square (centre), where the carriages and their escorts skirt past the Palace of Westminster (foreground) into Broad Sanctuary. This spacious thoroughfare connects the Houses of Parliament with Westminster Abbey, whose twin towers soar above the Victoria skyline to indicate the focus of the world's attention and curiosity. On the day, the Abbey is journey's end: in the longer term it provides life's starting point for Prince Andrew and his bride.

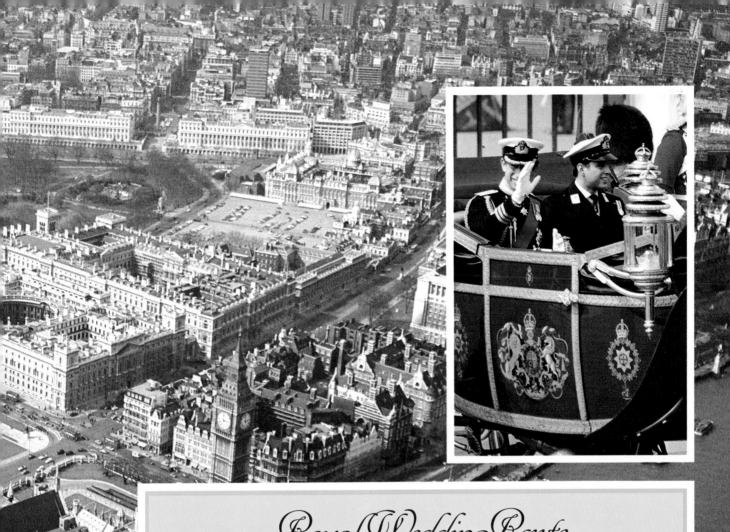

Royal Wedding Route

The royal route from Palace to Abbey is approximately 1 mile and 300 yards long – or about 1.8 kilometres. At the sedate trot appropriate to ceremonial processions of this kind, the entire journey can be comfortably covered in 12 minutes.

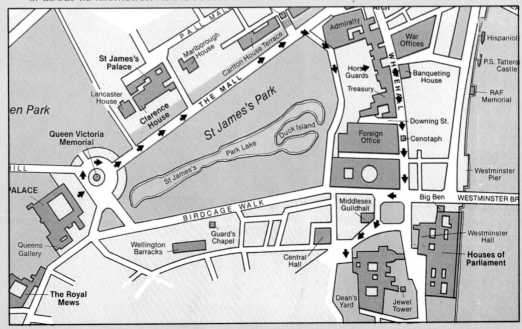

Admiralty
Arch
PALL MALL
Marlborough House
St James's Palace
Carlton House Terrace
War Offices
Hispaniola
P.S. Tatters Castle
Lancaster House
THE MALL
Horse Guards
Banqueting House
RAF Memorial
Clarence House
Treasury
WHITEHALL
en Park
Queen Victoria Memorial
St James's Park
Duck Island
Foreign Office
Downing St.
Cenotaph
St James's
Park Lake
HILL
Westminster Pier
PALACE
Middlesex Guildhall
Big Ben
WESTMINSTER BR
BIRDCAGE WALK
Queens Gallery
Guard's Chapel
Wellington Barracks
Westminster Hall
Central Hall
Houses of Parliament
The Royal Mews
Dean's Yard
Jewel Tower

JAMES VI and I
King of England, Scotland, France and Ireland
1566-1625

FREDERICK V *King of Bohemia & Elector Palatine of the Rhine* *1596-1632* =	**ELIZABETH** *1596-1662*	**CHARLES I** *King of Great Britain* *1600-1649* =	**HENRIETTA MARIA** *of France* *1609-1669*
ERNST AUGUST *Elector of Hanover* *1629-1698* =	**SOPHIA** *1630-1714*	**CHARLES II** *King of Great Britain* *1630-1685* ≠	**LUCY WALTERS** *daughter of Richard Walters* *1630-1658*
GEORGE I *King of Great Britain, France and Ireland* *1660-1727* =	**SOPHIA DOROTHEA** *of Brunswick-Luneburg & Celle* *1666-1726*	**JAMES CROFTS** *Duke of Monmouth* *1649-1685* =	**ANNE SCOTT** *Countess of Buccleuch* *1651-1732*
GEORGE II *King of Great Britain, France and Ireland* *1683-1760* =	**CAROLINE** *of Brandenburg-Ansbach* *1683-1737*	**JAMES** *Earl of Dalkeith* *1674-1705* =	**Lady HENRIETTA HYDE** *daughter of Laurence, Earl of Rochester* *Died 1730*
FREDERICK *Prince of Wales* *1707-1751* =	**AUGUSTA** *of Saxe-Coburg-Altenburg* *1719-1772*	**FRANCIS** *2nd Duke of Buccleuch* *1694-1751* =	**Lady JANE DOUGLAS** *daughter of the 2nd Duke of Queensberry* *Died 1729*
GEORGE III *King of Great Britain, France and Ireland* *1738-1820* =	**CHARLOTTE** *of Mecklenburg-Strelitz* *1744-1818*	**FRANCIS** *Earl of Dalkeith* *1720-1750* =	**Lady CAROLINE CAMPBELL** *daughter of John, 4th Duke of Argyll* *Died 1794*
EDWARD *Duke of Kent* *1767-1820* =	**VICTORIA MARY** *of Saxe-Coburg-Saalfeld* *1786-1861*	**HENRY** *3rd Duke of Buccleuch* *1746-1812* =	**ELIZABETH** *daughter of George, Duke of Montagu* *Died 1827*
VICTORIA *Queen of the United Kingdom of Great Britain and Ireland, and Empress of India* *1819-1901* =	**ALBERT** *of Saxe-Coburg-Gotha Prince Consort* *1819-1861*	**CHARLES** *4th Duke of Buccleuch* *1772-1819* =	**HARRIETT** *daughter of the 1st Viscount Sydney* *Died 1814*
EDWARD VII *King of the United Kingdom of Great Britain and Ireland* *1841-1910* =	**ALEXANDRA** *of Denmark* *1844-1925*	**WALTER** *5th Duke of Buccleuch* *1806-1884* =	**Lady CHARLOTTE THYNNE** *daughter of the 2nd Marquess of Bath* *Died 1895*
GEORGE V *King of the United Kingdom of Great Britain and Ireland* *1865-1936* =	**VICTORIA MARY** *of Teck* *1867-1953*	**WILLIAM** *6th Duke of Buccleuch* *1831-1914* =	**Lady LOUISA HAMILTON** *daughter of the 1st Duke of Abercorn* *Died 1912*
GEORGE VI *King of the United Kingdom of Great Britain and Ireland* *1895-1952* =	**Lady ELIZABETH BOWES-LYON** *Born 1900*	**Lord HERBERT MONTAGU-DOUGLAS-SCOTT** *1872-1944* =	**MARIE JOSEPHINE EDWARDS**
ELIZABETH II *Queen of the United Kingdom of Great Britain and Northern Ireland* *Born 1926* =	**PHILIP** *Duke of Edinburgh* *Born 1921*	**Colonel ANDREW FERGUSON** *1899-1966* =	**Hon MARIAN MONTAGU-DOUGLAS-SCOTT** *Born 1908*
		Major RONALD FERGUSON *Born 1931* =	**SUSAN WRIGHT** *Born 1937*

ANDREW Albert Christian Edward *Born 1960*

SARAH FERGUSON *Born 1959*

'I've got to get used to this "we" business!' exclaimed Prince Andrew, with his usual broad grin and happy-go-lucky chuckle. But there was a defensiveness in his smile, for he had just made – and not for the first time that morning – the cardinal mistake of referring to himself when he should have been referring to himself and his new fiancée. And his fiancée was sitting next to him.

They were talking about wedding plans, and he, after twenty-six years of being very much his own man, was being

consider himself to be on home ground. Had he been almost any other British mortal, he could that day have announced his engagement and simply proceeded to accomplish the business of a normal day. But as a prince of the blood royal and fourth in line to the throne of a thousand years, he now found himself confronting a succession of press, radio

(Left) Andrew's first official picture. (Below left) aged 4, with Grannie, and (below) a look through the family album with brother Edward and the Queen.

elbowed in the ribs every time he said 'I' when he should have said 'we'. And the lady responsible for the elbowing was determined to remind him in that way that, behind her own ready and irrepressible smile, it was 'we' from now on. Not the royal 'we' of course, for that went out of fashion long ago, except for official proclamations and Acts of Parliament, but the matrimonial 'we'. Right? Right!

Only in the sense that the conversation was taking place at Buckingham Palace could Prince Andrew

and television interviewers, photographers and cameramen and facing a barrage of questions about when, where and why the engagement had taken place at all, and what his (sorry, their) plans were for the immediate and long term future.

At first glance, it should not have been too difficult for someone already well accustomed to fielding interviewers' enquiries. But, like most royals who have submitted themselves to media scrutiny, Prince Andrew has always chosen to answer questions on subjects on which he might be described as an authority.

enjoying it all as a child enjoys its first outing to a funfair. Sitting straight-backed in the soft immensity of one of Buckingham Palace's less distinguished sofas (part of the furniture of Prince Andrew's suite of rooms), she parried the ammunition fired at her by her inquisitors, chipped in where Prince Andrew

faltered, giggled and fooled around as if unaware that on this of all occasions she would be heard and seen round the world, and generally gave the unmistakable impression that she was having a whale of a time, secure in the knowledge that it was better to have arrived than merely to travel.

(Right) Sarah at the Clapham home she shared before her engagement. (Above) the spacious Ferguson family home, heart of an 800-acre farming estate in the tiny Hampshire village of Dummer.

Unfortunately, there were no questions about helicopters here, nor about photography, nor about Gordonstoun, nor about the Falklands conflict. He was here to talk about a major change in his life and lifestyle, a future of which he could be certain of precious little, and a wife-to-be who kept digging him in the ribs every time he said 'I' instead of 'we'. No wonder he was a touch uneasy.

She, by contrast – the Sarah Ferguson whose name had been in every newspaper with increasing frequency for the best part of a year – seemed to be

Unlike Prince Andrew, who could not, even on this day, get out of the entrenched royal habit of striving for circumspection while giving serious, comprehensive and well-considered answers to weightier matters, Sarah was entirely self-possessed throughout, apologising only once – and then with a mischievous self-mockery – for not being serious enough, and leading everybody, including her future husband, to believe that she had no intention of being left out.

Even before the interview began, the couple were noticeably more relaxed. 'Where's the make-up?' joked the Prince, and Sarah nudged him as her freckled face broadened into unaffected laughter. She was wearing a sharply tailored navy blue wool suit with a wrap-over front giving a double-breasted effect, and an expansive shoulder line that might even

have made Princess Diana envious. The jacket was cinched in (as the jargon has it) above the waist by a deep, waist-hugging black belt, and complemented by an unpressed pleated skirt of spectacular length. Underneath the jacket she wore a simple, unadorned, round-necked blouse in vivid magenta crêpe-de-chine, while a matching ribbon bunched part of her huge mane of red hair. Sarah had bought the outfit only a couple of days before, from Alistair Blair, a 30-year-old up-and-coming fashion designer for whom Viscount Linley's girlfriend, Susannah Constantine, once worked as

(Left) Andrew celebrating the Queen Mother's 60th birthday with big brother and sister. (Below) family holiday at Balmoral in 1979. (Right) 8-year-old Andrew in the Marylebone Cub Scouts.

an assistant. That same week, as it happened, Blair had received standing ovations for his creations at the London Fashion Week shows. Sarah looked more than pleased that she had, unwittingly, picked a winner.

Two television interviewers were confident that they, too, had picked their own winner. Before long, their conversation with Andrew and his new-found bride-to-be became delightfully casual, rather more revealing, and easily as enjoyable as any royal interview in the twenty-five years or so since Prince Philip became the subject of the first tentative and respectful step to involve royalty in public conversation. In less than twenty minutes, Andrew and Sarah showed just how far the art had come since then.

Question: Congratulations to you, Sir, and best wishes to both of you. Could you tell us, please, first of all, how long ago

All the Queen's Men

On the average outdoor royal ceremonial occasion, the ranks of the Queen's Household Cavalry (consisting of the Life Guards and the Blues and Royals) outnumber her family by at least 100 to one! For full-scale royal weddings (like Prince Charles' in 1981, right) Sovereign's Escorts guard each and every carriage – so, despite the 2,000 or so uniformed servicemen lining the route, the day belongs very much to the Queen's personal bodyguard. She is their Colonel-in-Chief, and their opportunity to pay her tribute comes each year with Trooping the Colour (above). For Prince Andrew's wedding, they began training and rehearsals in April, already conscious that on the day itself they would have to be up at 4 a.m., with horses saddled, tacked and out of barracks before most Britons were even awake.

it was that you decided to marry?

Andrew: I asked Sarah some weeks ago, and Sarah actually said Yes, which...

Sarah: Surprising.

Andrew: ...surprised me. But she did say also... A little anecdote for you is that she said: 'If you wake up tomorrow morning you can tell me it's all a huge joke.' I didn't!

Engagement day for Andrew and Sarah. (Above) a quick kiss for the photographers. (Opposite) happy, contented, and patently relieved that their secret is out at last.

Sarah: So we're sitting here.

Question: So you started from a meeting at Ascot?

Andrew: Yes.

Question: And then everything developed from there in a way. When did you both know it was the real thing?

Andrew: Again, very difficult to answer, but I think that probably the end of last year, before Christmas, perhaps...

Sarah: Yes.

Andrew: And then it sort of...

Sarah: ...carried on from there.

Andrew: Carried on from there after

Christmas at Sandringham, and then beyond that.

Question: What first impressions did you have of one another then, in that case?

Sarah: Very good friends.

Andrew: (a) Very good friends, and (b) it was at lunch – wasn't it? – that...

Sarah: Yes.

Andrew: ...we were made to sit next door to each other at Ascot.

Sarah: Yes, and he made me eat chocolate profiteroles, which I didn't want to eat at all.

Andrew: I then didn't have any. So I got hit.

Sarah: Very hard!

Andrew: And it started from there. I think that's probably where it...

Sarah: I was meant to be on a diet.

Question: And that was the basis of a romance?

Sarah: Yes.

Andrew: There are always humble beginnings. It's got to start somewhere. But, I mean, we've known each other since we were four or five – perhaps not knowingly since four or five – until, again, about 1983 when we were staying at various house parties together around

the country during the part of '83 and '84, and it was at Ascot that, as it were, the whole thing, as you say, took off. And it wasn't at Ascot as such that we realised that there was anything in it. It was later on.

Sarah: Yes.

Question: I think you said, Sir, that when you met the right girl, it would probably come like a lightning bolt.

Andrew: You're not the first person who's asked me this question today. In fact there are about three or four other people who've asked it. And I'm really at a loss to say... I mean, I don't think that Sarah is a thunderbolt.

Sarah: Nor am I a streak of lightning. Nor is he, I don't think.

Question: Can I ask you if you can tell us what you like about each other?

Andrew: Oh!

Sarah: Wit. Charm.

Andrew: Yes, probably.

Sarah: Yes.

Andrew: And the red hair.

Sarah: And the good looks! (**Pulls a face, slaps Andrew on the leg, and laughs.**) Sorry!

Question: Could we...?

Andrew: I'm watching carefully! Go on.

Question: Could we perhaps now have a rather more lingering look at the ring? I mean, how did you find time to – or the secrecy, the away-from-the-media-ness – to go out and buy it?

Andrew: Well, very fortunately I didn't actually have to go out and buy. Somebody very kindly came in with some suggestions, and it was made very kindly by some very nice engineers, I think.

Sarah: Engineers?

Andrew: I don't think they'd like to be called engineers, but...

Sarah: Definitely not!

Andrew: ...I don't know what you'd call them.

Sarah: Jewellers!

Andrew: Jewellers.

Question: Miss Ferguson, how would you describe that lovely ring?

Sarah: Stunning. Red – I wanted a ruby. Well, I didn't want it – I'm very lucky to have it. But certainly it's a lovely stone. And I've got red hair too.

Andrew: It was... again, it's something that we discussed in the last few weeks, and

we came to the mutual conclusion that red was probably the best colour for Sarah. And that's how we came to the choice of the ruby. And then the extra bits round the outside – we wanted something that was slightly unconventional, and I think we've got something there.

Sarah: Yes, very original. I think Andrew – you actually designed it, didn't you?

Andrew: Er, I helped in the design.

Question: What, you mean with sketches and things?

Andrew: Well, we did sketch some of it, and I found a suggestion in another selection of rings that I was given, and then I asked them to check... I'm not quite sure what the shape of the original was that I drew, but they looked like rugby balls – little tiny ones – and these are drops rather than rugby balls.

Sarah: Thank goodness for that! I'd hate to wear a rugby ball round my hand.

Question: Can you tell us about the proposal – where and when it took place?

Andrew: It was some weeks ago, staying privately in Scotland. And I'd go no further than saying that.

Question: Could I ask you then, Miss Ferguson, do you remember what he said?

Sarah: Absolutely. But I'm not telling you!

Question: Did he go down on one knee in the approved fashion?

Andrew: No, both. That I will tell you. Both.

Sarah: Yes, both.

Question: And you, of course, very formally asked your prospective father-in-law for Miss Ferguson's hand in marriage?

Andrew: Yes, that was also fairly nerve-racking, knowing Major Ronald from a long time ago, at the polo. And I asked him this week-end, as well as Her Majesty.

Question: What was the Queen's reaction?

Andrew: Overjoyed. Very happy, very pleased. And beyond that, I think that – what else? – I mean, just as a delighted parent, I think.

Sarah: As indeed is my father.

Question: There was no phrase using the words 'settling down' when she said 'Congratulations'?

Profile

Name: Sarah Margaret Ferguson
Date of birth: October 15, 1959
Place of birth: London
Father: Major Ronald Ferguson
Mother: Mrs Susan Barrantes (formerly Ferguson, née Wright)
Sister: Jane, born 1957, married (to Alex Makin) with 1 daughter
Stepmother: Mrs Susan Ferguson
Half-brother and sisters: Andrew (7), Alice (5), Eliza (b. 1985)
Family Home: Dummer Down Farm, near Basingstoke, Hampshire
Schools: (1) Daneshill Prep School, Basingstoke; (2) Hurst Lodge, Sunningdale, Berkshire
Qualifications: 6 'O' Levels, 2 CSEs
Career: Worked for flat-letting agency; art dealer; sports PR agency; graphic arts company.
Height: 5' 9"
Colour of hair: Auburn-red
Colour of eyes: Hazel

Andrew: How do you mean, 'settling down'?

Question: Well, becoming a married man...

Andrew: Oh, Gosh! I see; that way.

Question: ...and responsibilities thereby.

Andrew: No, no. I mean, I don't see there's anything settling in it. It's a mighty upheaval for most people, and I think it'll be an upheaval for both of us in terms of we've both got to come to terms (a) with life as it will continue...

Sarah: We're a good team, anyway.

Andrew: Yes. I think that's the saving grace, the fact that in the last nine months we've discovered that we work very well together.

Sarah: We're good friends; a good team. Quite happy... very happy.

Question: Miss Ferguson, could I ask you, how do you think you're going to cope with this new role and at the same time being a Navy wife?

Sarah: I'm going to enjoy it immensely. I think I'm going to cope with the help of Andrew here.

Andrew: I think it's worth saying that I have no plans to change my Navy career, on the advice of Sarah.

Sarah: Very strongly.

Andrew: We discussed it at some length, and for the foreseeable future I will be continuing my naval career as it is at the moment. Sarah is quite prepared to put up with that, and I think that she will be a remarkable wife if she can. And I know how difficult it is – talking to naval colleagues of mine – what it's like to be married to a naval officer, because we do spend such a long time away.

Sarah: Also, I've got a job to do, too. And I'm going to keep on working, and... So I think it's going to be very good.

Question: You think it will be possible to keep on working...

Sarah: Absolutely.

Question: ...with the pressures that...

Sarah: Absolutely.

Question: ...tend to apply?

Sarah: My job is a printing and publishing job, therefore I have the freedom to... and

(Right) Sarah, the bride-to-be. (Left) her father, Ronald, with the Prince of Wales: Major Ferguson is Charles' polo manager.

since I work for myself I have the freedom to, sort of, arrange things round what I can do. So I can do a bit of everything, really.

Andrew: I think it's a great advantage in being almost self-employed and working for somebody outside the country and running an office over here, in that Sarah's (a) her own boss here, so she can make her own work schedules up to suit herself, and she knows that there are times when she has to go to work, therefore she can go to work.

Sarah: Mmm. So when Andrew's away I will work harder than perhaps when Andrew's here. Right? Right.

Andrew: Hopefully.

Question: Have you, in the course of this rather difficult last month or so had any advice from the Prince and Princess of Wales, who went through much the same thing?

Sarah: The Princess of Wales and I are extremely good friends and we naturally talk about a lot of different subjects.

Question: Like dealing with the media?

Andrew the traveller: (left) recently returned from Canada; (below) in the States; (below right) home from the Falklands; (far right) boarding a wartime fighter.

Profile

Name: Andrew Albert Christian Edward Mountbatten-Windsor
Date of birth: February 19, 1960
Place of birth: Buckingham Palace
Father: HRH Prince Philip
Mother: HM Queen Elizabeth II
Brothers: (1) HRH The Prince of Wales; (2) HRH Prince Edward
Sister: HRH Princess Anne
Family homes: Windsor Castle, Buckingham Palace, Sandringham, Balmoral Castle Schools:
Heatherdown Preparatory School, Berkshire; Gordonstoun; Lakefield College, Ontario
Qualifications: 6 'O' Levels, 3 'A' Levels
Career: Began 12-year Royal Navy commission in 1979 as helicopter pilot. Saw action in the Falklands
and is now a Lieutenant
Height: 5' 11"
Colour of hair: Dark brown
Colour of eyes: Blue

Sarah: Lots of different subjects.

Andrew: Yes, I think that's possibly the best way of answering that. I mean, there...

Sarah: We're very, very good friends.

Andrew: ...there are so many different, differing ideas about how to handle yourself that you can't take one person's advice all the time.

Sarah: Although there is no-one better than the Princess of Wales.

Question: The plans for the wedding are by no means final – in fact, you don't even know when or where.

Andrew: No.

Question: What sort of wedding would you like to have?

Andrew: Er – as in red, white or blue? No. I hope a London wedding, and I hope a white wedding. Sarah is already charging around looking for a dress – or looking for ideas. Beyond that, I have absolutely no idea.

Sarah: You've got your dress?

Andrew: Yes, I've got my dress, thank you.

Lindsey Walton
ENG. Frank Golding

Yes. I'm not so sure that it would fit. But anyway, the plans are still up in the air because now of course we go on into the planning stage and the summer schedule is a very tight one, and I would very much like it to be in the summer – and so would Sarah. Sarah more so because I think that...

Sarah: Mmm – get on with it.

Andrew: Get on with it and get it out of the way. Because of course the summer schedule's very tight this year and I would hope some time perhaps in July or August. If it's not possible to do it in July or August, then I think...

Sarah: We would, yes.

Andrew: Sorry – we: I've got to get used to this 'we' business.

Sarah: I know, it's difficult, isn't it? We – OK?

Andrew: We. That's right.

Sarah: Right.

Andrew: Otherwise the fall-back is sometime in the autumn.

Question: It has been a bit of a whirlwind, hasn't it, really? You've only known each other for – what is it? – nine months?

Sarah: Definitely not!

Question: No?

Andrew: I certainly wouldn't consider it a whirlwind at all. It may be a whirlwind to some people because, of course, I suppose that the media only discovered about it in...

Sarah: In January.

Andrew: ...in January/December, just after Christmas, but...

Sarah: In fact, there's...

Andrew: ...there's quite a lot that went on before. In fact more than what went on after.

Question: What are your plans between now and the wedding?

Sarah: Hard work.

Andrew: Hard work. I've got a course to do.

Sarah: I've got a job to do.

Andrew: So we shall be getting on with it. The course that I'm going to do finishes as the beginning of June, so I will have the time to sit down and plan the wedding and the arrangements afterwards.

Question: Looking towards the future a little, you come from – both of you – from fairly large families. Would you like to repeat that pattern? Would you like to have quite a lot of children?

Andrew: I don't know really. I mean... (**To Sarah**) What do you say?

Sarah: Don't know. What do you say?

Andrew: I think that we haven't actually... I mean, that's something that – until we get married – that we haven't, sort of, thought about. There is an awful lot to think about in the next – whatever it is – until we get married.

Sarah: Quite fun to have quite a few, anyway.

Andrew: I agree, it would be quite fun.

Sarah: Umm...

Andrew: You can answer that one!

Sarah: I'm going to! How do I feel about my new title? Er – what's the word?

Andrew: Change of name?

Sarah: Change of name. A great honour. Much looking forward to carrying it out, whatever I'm supposed to do. That's it, I think.

Question: Do you think, in public terms, that they'll have rather a hard job getting

Despite their different backgrounds, the Fergusons are no strangers to the Windsors. There are distant blood ties, but more recently the Royal Family's interest in polo brought them together over twenty years ago.

But, again, number, size and all the rest of it is still way, way in the future, and really it's not possible...

Sarah: It has yet to be decided.

Question: Notionally, it's a good idea, though?

Andrew: Yes.

Question: Can I put a final question to you, Miss Ferguson? How do you feel about your new title, because after your marriage you'll be known as Princess Andrew?

all the way from Fergie to Princess Andrew?

Sarah: No.

Question: I mean, you've caught the affection over the past few months as Fergie: suddenly Princess Andrew seems a bit of a mouthful.

Andrew: It's not all that sudden. You have got time to acclimatise to it. I mean, we are talking of some months away.

Sarah: You could find a nickname around Princess Andrew!

Statistics for the 'Big Day'

Considering that even royal wedding ceremonies last only for an hour, the involvement of time, money and manpower is monumental. Television audiences world wide amount to over 750 million, almost a thousand times the number of spectators who line the route for a glimpse of the royal couple, and 400,000 times as many as the number of wedding guests. An army of florists, hairdressers, cosmeticians, valets and maids have to be up before daybreak to attend to bride and groom, rivalling for early rising another army of photographers, journalists, television cameramen and radio commentators all wrestling with sheafs of notes and hundreds of miles of cable in the half-light of dawn. Unsolicited wedding gifts number up to 10,000, of which about 3,000 are kept and a few hundred exhibited publicly. Among the gifts there are normally a good dozen wedding cakes, in addition to the official one measuring some four feet high, weighing between one and two hundredweight, and sufficient to feed over a thousand. But the wedding breakfast is comparatively modest: less than a hundred guests – closest family only. And only one toast, drunk in silence, with no speeches.

Andrew: Mmm – yes, well all right... But I'm not going to help, though!

Question: May I, on behalf of ITN and the BBC, offer you our best wishes and all happiness for the future.

Andrew: Thank you very much.

Sarah: Thank you very much indeed.

With that, the biggest hurdle that life had thus far placed before Sarah Ferguson was successfully cleared. Like most stories in which the sort of everyday girl you would not particularly notice in a crowd is met, wooed and won by a prince, that morning's events were a far cry in time and circumstance from the early autumn day in 1959 when she first saw the light, if not of day, then of a delivery room at a nursing home in Welbeck Street in London's West End.

Sarah Margaret Ferguson was born on 15th October, 1959. At the time, and barely half a mile away, Her Majesty Queen Elizabeth II was in the fifth month of her third pregnancy – which would result in the birth of Prince Andrew the following February. Little did Sarah's parents suspect how significant the two events would turn out to be for both

Prince Andrew does not play polo, but first met Sarah while watching a match in which both their fathers played at Smith's Lawn, Windsor Great Park, in 1965. Since Prince Charles took up the game, Andrew has been a frequent spectator – Sarah too, since her close friend Princess Diana first took an interest, and since her father became Vice Chairman of Guards Polo Club.

Family connection: Charles and Diana chat with Sarah's father (below right) at Windsor in 1982. (Left) horseplay between brothers – was Sarah watching?

infants and their families.

There was little reason to put two and two together in those early days. Though the Fergusons can claim all manner of royal connections in their complex and sometimes quite aristocratic family tree, they were very much on the fringes of royal acquaintance. Sarah's father, Major Ronald Ivor Ferguson, now retired from the Life Guards, once commanded the Sovereign's Escort of the Household Cavalry – they nicknamed him 'the General' as a result – and this had brought him into close contact with the Queen in the early years of her reign. He became the driving force behind (and is now Vice-Chairman of) Guards Polo Club, the association which Prince Philip and later Prince Charles were to join, but the early personal ties between Windsors and Fergusons were at best tenuous.

For Ronald Ferguson, these were the prime years of family life. He had been married in his early twenties to Susan Wright, an attractive teenager with a personality which, though precociously strong, matched her husband's liking for straight talk and direct action. Despite the six years' difference in their ages, the marriage blossomed and within four years the couple were the parents of two daughters.

Sarah may have laughed and smiled on her engagement day, and (although from the few early family photographs so

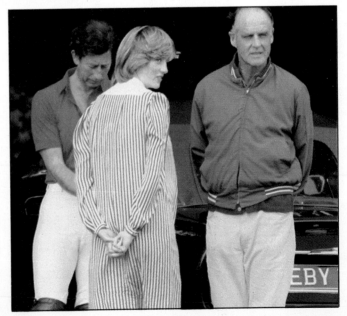

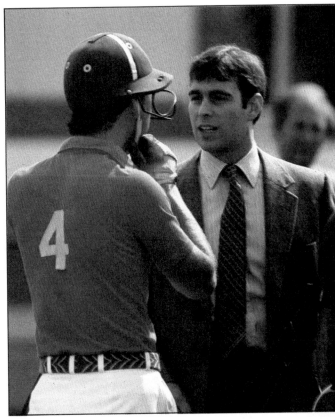

Diana has become a firm polo enthusiast – (right) spectating only three weeks before Prince William was born. Sarah looks like following suit.

far released publicly, and which show her as rather serious and self-effacing, apparently reluctant to be photographed at all, it might seem that this was not always so) she appears to have been laughing and smiling almost since the day of her birth. She was, in the words of her father, 'a very good child, always cheerful and full of fun.'

She was brought up on an 800-acre farming estate (now said to have a capital value of £2 million) just outside the village of Dummer, near Basingstoke in the north-east of Hampshire.

But the pleasure Sarah derived from her expansive home stamping-ground was purely domestic, and she became well-known by the three hundred or so inhabitants of the tiny, picturesque village for her bright, bubbling good nature. 'A jolly, sprightly girl who makes me laugh and can take a joke herself,' the

church caretaker said of Sarah, while the chairman of the local parish council praised the way she and her sister were brought up to 'talk to the cowman and ploughman in the same polite way as they would to members of titled families.'

As if aware that she would one day be a member of the Royal Family, she took to horses at the royally early age of three. For stimulus and encouragement in this field she has her mother to thank: Susan Ferguson was not only an excellent and competent horsewoman herself, but also very anxious that her children should share her enthusiasm for this pastime. Sarah let no grass grow under her feet, graduating from Pony Club events to gymkhanas, then junior trials, with determination and speed, eagerly collecting shelvesful of cups, trophies and rosettes along the way. Sometimes she was rather too eager, showing a tendency to tank hell-for-leather towards fences and obstacles, and finishing up horseless, a crashed bundle of frustration furiously walloping the ground with her crop for all she was worth.

A Royal Family

A country girl at heart, Sarah will feel very much at home with her in-laws. Though they show their emotions in public only rarely (as on Andrew's homecoming from the Falklands, above), they form a close and affectionate family unit within the privacy of their country homes – Windsor Castle, Sandringham, Balmoral, Highgrove and the Castle of Mey. Buckingham Palace has rarely been regarded as 'home' by royalty. It is at Windsor that the Queen prefers to spend her family weekends and which she opens to all her relations at Christmas. Sandringham (top left) offers the immediate family a New Year's break during the pheasant-shooting season. Balmoral (far left) provides a remote Scottish retreat where the Queen, her children and grandchildren spend long summer weeks. They usually travel there in the Royal Yacht, which almost invariably stops at Scrabster so that everyone can call in on the Queen Mother at her Castle of Mey (left) – one of the happiest family reunions of the year. Andrew and Sarah will have the use of all these homes, but for real privacy they may choose to stay in any of the outlying lodges and cottages, just as Charles and Diana spend weekends at Sandringham's Wood Farm, or Craigowan Lodge on the Balmoral estate.

Her education was a comparatively mild business. At the age of five she went off to her first school – Daneshill, near Basingstoke – which, then as now, catered for around 200 children, and which Sarah's half-brother, seven-year-old Andrew and half-sister Alice, aged five, now attend. Her headmistress, Miss June Vallance, singled her out as a great sports fiend with courage to spare. She

as light-hearted as it may seem. In 1973, when Sarah was only thirteen, her mother left home to share her life with an Argentinian professional polo player, Hector Barrantes. Predictably, Susan's departure and the divorce proceedings that followed it were traumatic: 'a bit of a fright, to put it mildly, for everyone,' said Ronald later. Neither Sarah nor her sister had suspected what might happen, and it

was left to their father to break the news to them after the event. 'I don't know how I told them that their mother had gone,' he said. 'I just know the feeling, knowing that she'd left me with two girls.' For Jane it was a time of terrible insecurity, and she drew close to Sarah as few older sisters do.

Sarah herself was deeply upset by her mother's disappearance, but did not

The Ring

Sarah's engagement ring consists of a single, large Burmese ruby set amid ten drop diamonds, on a band of white and yellow gold. Made by Garrards, the Queen's jewellers, it is reputed to be worth at least £25,000. Prince Andrew helped to design the ring, and the couple chose the ruby because Sarah has red hair.

proved a reasonably successful all-rounder in class, though with no great academic promise.

By the time she settled in at secondary school – the exclusive, small, red-brick Hurst Lodge at Sunningdale in Berkshire – she had gathered round her a large complement of friends and evolved a mature and sympathetic personality. It was because of this, because of her adult sense of responsibility, her helpfulness and sense of organisation, that in 1976, her final year, she was chosen as head girl.

'We have so many girls coming and going that it is easy to forget them,' said one of her teachers, 'but nobody ever forgot Sarah.' Nor did she leave without qualifications: she picked up six 'O' levels – in Art, English Language, English Literature, Spoken English, French and Biology – and CSEs in Maths and Geography. But she never pursued her academic education further. 'What? 'A' levels?' she once said. 'You must be joking!'

Not all of her school career had been

A ring (above) and a kiss (opposite) signify the end of Andrew's eligible bachelorhood. (Right) enjoying a dinner dance in America's Cup Week, 1983.

react openly, and bravely hid her feelings. Her teachers vouch for the fact that they would have known nothing about it had they not been informed officially, and her father found her much more readily adaptable to a home life lacking the pivot of a wife and mother. This may have been primarily because, being a weekly boarder at Hurst Lodge, her day-by-day existence changed very little, but on the other hand, Major Ronald's contribution was probably incalculable. Aware of his daughters' vulnerability, and knowing in his heart of hearts that 'it doesn't matter what the father is like or how much he

takes upon himself, or what he does, there is no substitute whatever for a mother at that age', he strove to to his best.

Fortunately, he had the steel to cope with the situation, and he was blest with daughters who were fundamentally easy-going. But he was determined to keep what remained of the family as a unit, and to see that Sarah was not embittered by the experience. That was not easy, with some so-called family friends drifting off and withdrawing their support for fear of being tainted by the whiff of scandal, and with a wife who was content to dispense advice to him without having the responsibility of carrying it out in practice. So there was, as he admitted, 'the odd trying moment, but I hope the girls never realised how tough it was.'

It is a sign of the maturity of the daughter as well as proof that time can heal, that Sarah still feels very close to her mother even though they see each other only rarely. The two get on extremely well together, despite the understandable and irreversible change in their relationship in the last dozen years or so. But, while sister Jane's sense of dependence led to an early marriage – at the age of eighteen she married another polo player, Alex Makim, and the couple went off to farm in Australia – Sarah, being of younger years, had to rely almost solely on her father. Their respect and admiration for each other dates from this time, and Ronald is quietly gratified these days that 'we talk about everything and, of course, she consults me.'

She will probably always be grateful to him for never having attempted to compensate for the domestic upheaval by spoiling her. Never an over-indulgent father, he was aware that to spend his way out of the trials of readjustment would merely have added a mistaken set of values and priorities to the uncertainty that Sarah undoubtedly felt then. For all his protective affection for her he knew that there was no time like the present for teaching her, as he put it, 'to stand on her own two feet'.

(Opposite) Sarah, the latest royal Sloane, may have to give up her liking for the loose, casual, wrap-round look.

'... The Stars in their Courses'

SARAH (*Libra*)

This marriage brings Sarah radical lifestyle changes just when her mental development will accelerate tremendously. Her Sun in Libra and Moon in Aries show that personal relations are important, that she demands an active part in making decisions and strives to live up to public expectations. Librans being keen on beauty and fashion, her appearance will change sharply with advice from top designers. She and Andrew are both strong-willed with their own ideas on how to live life, but chart comparisons indicate harmonious solutions to problems. They will never be bored together. Children will prove a great joy, and though Sarah is not exactly motherly, she will be actively concerned to ensure their upbringing and education in a protected, peaceful environment.

ANDREW (*Pisces*)

Andrew was born exactly on the Aquarius/Pisces cusp combining a need for independence and a love of the untried with warm-hearted sympathy. In this marriage of love and mutual romantic attraction, he will not find it easy to accept restrictions and will continue to surprise by unconventional, even rebellious actions. A sensitive, creative person seeking positive ways of self-expression, he will be an attentive, loving husband, protective of Sarah, and concerned for her well-being. His playful, mischievous nature will never cease to amuse and amaze her, and his children (at least two) will be very lucky to have him as a father. He likes to be in charge, but Sarah, who likes to organise and knows her own mind, will find ways of getting what she wants.

He clearly succeeded, for less than three years after his divorce, he felt able to marry again. His second wife was another Susan – former debutante Susan Deptford – and the daughter of a Cambridgeshire farmer. Over fifteen years Ronald's junior (and only twelve years older than Sarah), she proved the ideal stepmother. She ploughed no furrows of her own, accepted the fact that, in any household, two teenage stepdaughters might prove an obstacle to a trouble-free marriage, and adopted a low profile. Placid and understanding by nature, she found it easy to listen to Sarah's adolescent woes and to help her through the problems of growing up. By the time Jane had married and Sarah, having reached her eighteenth birthday, was on the look-out for a job, Ronald and Susan decided to start a family of their own.

In her search for employment, Sarah went straight to Queen's Secretarial College in Kensington where, although she was found to be 'a bit slapdash' at times, she impressed by her ready acceptance of responsibility,

Andrew, latest in a long line of Navy royals, at Dartmouth's 1980 passing out parade (below); two years later (left and below right) he returns home safely on HMS Invincible from the Falklands.

Senior Service

The Royal Family's Navy links go back to Henry VII, who developed it in the 15th century. Henry VIII strengthened it; Elizabeth I secured England's freedom with it. Charles II and James II were devoted to the sea and ships, while George III's brother and two sons (William IV and Queen Victoria's father) served in the Navy. Victoria's, Edward VII's and George V's second sons all chose naval careers, as did Prince Philip, his Mountbatten uncle and grandfather.

demonstrated that she had initiative, and charmed by a personality which, they said, 'she will well use to her advantage when she gets older.' Subsequent employers were inclined to agree. A Covent Garden art dealer for whom she worked in 1981 confirmed that she did everything with great energy and tremendous speed, while Peter Cunard, the head of a sports public relations agency where she was later employed, found her so keen to get things done that she was always prepared to work late when necessary. What was more, she was never afraid of anybody, and was always 'up front'.

She also worked for a small flat-letting agency in Knightsbridge, but since 1984 has been a member of the firm of BCK, a graphic arts publishing company in Mayfair's George Street – an area much favoured by younger members of the Royal Family in their search for careers. Her responsibilities included assembling catalogues and publicity material, and the company's director, Richard Burton, soon found that she could cope with the job with the minimum of supervision, and that since all she needed was a desk, a telephone and a little direction from the boss, she could in fact work quite easily from home.

Home for Sarah, the working girl, was a chintzy, two-bedroom flat, part of an

its three storeys shielded by unpretentious net curtains. Sarah shared the flat with one of her few firm friends, Carolyn Beckwith-Smith, a cousin of the Princess of Wales' senior Lady-in-Waiting. Coincidentally, Carolyn herself was already engaged to an Old Etonian, Harry Cotterell, who runs a laundry valet service in Chelsea.

Sarah's social life was as busy as her workdays, and hardly suffered from her increasing work-load. In fact, one of her employers was later to recall that she used to spend an inordinate amount of time on the telephone arranging all sorts of evenings and weekends with her friends. It was typical Sloane Ranger behaviour – a stream of social contacts,

Though she wants to continue being a working woman, Sarah will soon get to know how royalty works so that she can join Andrew on official engagements.

Edwardian terraced house in Lavender Gardens, Clapham. A longish, typically turn-of-the-century suburban street, Lavender Gardens is squeezed parallel with a dozen others between the main A3 road into Central London and the film-famous Lavender Hill, equidistant from Clapham Junction to the north-west and Clapham Common to the south-east.

The house – number 40 – is unexceptional, the dull tint of its outer walls brightened by the occasional artistic flourish of stone carvings and loud red-brick dressings, and the windows of never-ending ideas for living life to the full, and endless gossip about people, places and fashion. She and her fellow Sloanes searched out the best – or at least, the most fashionable – restaurants and discos, and trailed round the fashion houses and stores of Knightsbridge and

A Day for Celebration

Royal weddings bring the opportunity for celebrations that are both official and informal. Gun salutes at the Tower of London and in Hyde Park, the raising of Union Jacks on all public buildings, and the playing of the National Anthem on radio and television have always characterised the official form of rejoicing. But more memorable for most of us are the streets hung with banners and bunting, the shop windows plastered with flags and messages of congratulation, those huge street parties, and the wealth of souvenirs – wedding mugs, goblets, plates, busts, plaques, medallions, coins, stamps, jigsaw puzzles, playing cards and so on. Londoners and visitors claiming overnight sleeping plots on the royal route traditionally celebrate right through the night before the wedding – as they did for Prince Charles in 1981 – providing a welcome oasis of fun and good humour.

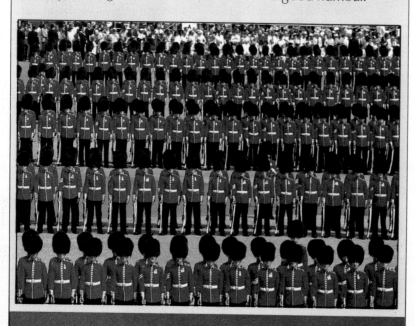

Chelsea for clothes in the very best Diana Spencer tradition.

It was not, however, an irresponsible, spendthrift existence. Sarah's father was at pains to point out that, in line with his policy of not spoiling her, he gave her only a meagre allowance – 'and when I say meagre, I mean meagre' – to top up a modest income from a trust which his own father set up for his granddaughters. Sarah's weekends did not have to be

Sporting Life

Like many members of the Royal Family, Sarah enjoys ski-ing: it was her appearance at Klosters with Charles and Diana that fuelled rumours of her engagement to Andrew. She has also enjoyed the royal pastime of horse-riding since the age of 3, and as a girl took part in Pony Club events, junior trials and gymkhanas. Andrew's sporting horizons are broader: at school he played hockey and rugby and took part in athletics: today he likes sailing and shooting and will occasionally try his luck at cricket. Like Sarah, he is a keen skier – and they both love disco-dancing. And Andrew's artistic flair for photography is matched by Sarah's work in graphic arts.

expensive affairs: she was always welcome back home at Dummer Down Farm, where her stepsister and brother (a third child – Eliza – was born to Ronald and Susan in 1985) found, and still find, her an indulgent, fun companion. Meanwhile, on the social front, she enjoyed enough friendships of the right kind to be invited to house-parties all over Britain in the comfortable country houses of well-to-do and well-connected families.

In June 1985 she was invited to the

most prestigious house-party of all – the Queen's week-long family-and-friends gathering at Windsor Castle during Ascot Week. Guards Polo Club, as it normally does, ran a three-day tournament at Windsor during the same week, and Major Ronald was there as usual watching his protege, Prince Charles, play. So in a sense it was natural that Sarah should, for once, be invited to join the Queen as the daughter of a family friend. Added to which, of course, she was a close friend of the Queen's daughter-in-law – a fact which was later to give rise to the erroneous story that Diana played Cupid from then onwards.

No-one has yet claimed or admitted responsibility for seating Sarah next to Prince Andrew at dinner, but that now famous mock spat over who should eat the profiteroles became what Andrew later described as 'the humble beginning' for a romance. He didn't know it then, or indeed for another six months. In fact, when he was interviewed one afternoon in September for the radio programme *Woman's Hour*, he declared that there was no-one on the horizon as a future wife, but that when he met the girl he wanted to marry, he would know immediately – it would hit him like a lightning bolt.

The question of his marriage was nothing if not timely for, by then, Andrew was well past his twenty-fifth birthday – and hence he was no longer obliged to seek the Queen's consent to marry. Perhaps for that reason, his 25th birthday had been loudly hailed the previous February, the congratulations and speculation being accompanied by long and sometimes nostalgic backward glances over his comparatively short, but certainly eventful life.

Naturally, his birth was heralded, announced and welcomed in circumstances very different from those in which Sarah came into the world. For four days before his arrival, quite large crowds hugged the railings of Buckingham Palace in a loyal attempt to be there when the news was given. One man brought with him a portable record player, complete with a recording of *Land*

of *Hope and Glory* to play on it when the announcement came.

On a more mundane level, the British public were speculating on whether the new Prince, born at 3.30 on a sleety February afternoon, would be given the title of Duke of York, whether President Eisenhower would be one of his godfathers, or whether the Queen would draw the 18/- (90p) family allowance to which she was now entitled. No, said Buckingham Palace to that one

The names for the new baby had been hotly guessed at since well before the birth. If Andrew was floated at all, it came a long, long way down everybody's list, well after the Alberts, Jameses and Edwards. True to a tradition which has

Queen – justifying the oft-quoted description, 'radiant' – holding a fine, contented infant and surrounded by husband and children looking proud and happy, and it became an immediate classic among royal portfolios.

At the beginning of August, Andrew's grandmother, Queen Elizabeth the Queen Mother, celebrated her sixtieth birthday. The anniversary provoked the sort of rash of eulogies to which we have all become accustomed in each of the years following her 70th birthday, but it lacked the vaguely official character that, for instance, characterised the Queen's own sixtieth birthday in April 1986. And in keeping with the domestic nature of the occasion, the Queen Mother invited her

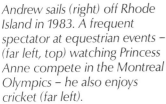

Andrew sails (right) off Rhode Island in 1983. A frequent spectator at equestrian events – (far left, top) watching Princess Anne compete in the Montreal Olympics – he also enjoys cricket (far left).

now happily been discontinued, it was not until over a month after his birth that his names were announced. They were Andrew (after Prince Philip's father, Prince Andrew of Greece), Albert (after the Queen's father, known as Prince Albert until he became Duke of York in 1920), Christian (after King Christian IX of Denmark, the great-great grandfather of both the Queen and Prince Philip), and Edward (after King Edward VII). In those days when relations between the Royal

Family and the exiled Duke of Windsor were a matter of frequent controversy, it did not take long for someone to point out that all of Prince Andrew's names were also borne by the former King Edward VIII, and to wonder whether this was not tempting fate!

With the announcement of the names came an album of 'official' photographs, taken by Cecil Beaton a few days earlier in the Music room of Buckingham Palace. It was a delightful selection, showing the

grandchildren Charles and Anne to Clarence House to have their pictures taken with her. At the last moment, the Queen thought it would be nice to send the baby along too, and so young Andrew found himself wriggling on the Queen Mother's knee as the photographer snapped away. Gummy smiles, curling toes, blond fluffy hair – this was the stuff to put into a nation's newspapers next morning.

Barring another set of family

A bright hour on a damp day: Andrew and Sarah, now engaged, in the garden of Buckingham Palace.

photographs taken the following month, with Andrew joining the Queen, Prince Philip and their elder children on a tartan plaid rug spread out on the lawn of Balmoral Castle, public sightings of Andrew were few and far between. Opportunities were limited to family holidays, when train journeys to or from Scotland and Sandringham offered a glimpse of the Prince and excuse for speculating on his progress. Though this low-key exposure was well-meant, it tended to backfire at times when, for want of positive proof of his good health, the lack of first-hand information was taken as an indication that there might just be (in the tactful phraseology of the time) 'something wrong' with the Queen's third child.

Eventually, people came to terms with the prospect of seeing very little of their young prince. With busy parents, and siblings ten or more years older than he,

his life at Buckingham Palace was hardly enviable, for all the comfort and material security it offered, but he was soon able to enjoy the company of a virtual platoon of cousins, as first Princess Margaret, then Princess Alexandra, then the Duchess of Kent, married and had children. And in 1964 – the Year of the Royal Babies – his mother presented him with a baby brother. From then on, with the veneer of responsibility for young Prince Edward, Andrew seems to have become a more self-assured youngster.

As his elder brother and sister temporarily disappeared from the scene into their private schools, Andrew seemed to emerge into public consciousness. Whether tricked out in emerald green velvet as page-boy at the Marquess of Hamilton's wedding at the age of six, or watching work on the new Hovercraft on the Isle of Wight two years later, he was at last seen with satisfying

frequency and, more important, in an acceptable light.

The year 1968 seems to have been something of a turning point. In it, he joined the First Marylebone Cub Scout pack, emulating the sense of service in early age which had led Princess Anne into the Brownies. He was taken to several public and ceremonial events at Windsor, and royal sporting outings – polo, Braemar, the Windsor Horse Show – soon seemed incomplete without him. In September the Queen and Duke of Edinburgh took him to his first school, Heatherdown, near Ascot, where he was met in the full glare of media publicity by the headmaster in the school grounds. Oddly, the snapping of cameras failed to

unnerve him: suited in regulation charcoal grey with light blue shirt and scarlet tie and cap, Andrew fairly oozed confidence, seeming to take the whole occasion so much in his stride that it augured well for his immediate future.

Naturally, life was very different from his previous educational existence. Here was no governess to teach him basic subjects in an exclusive class of four or five relatives and friends, but a rota of masters detailed to treat him like hundreds of other boys, drive knowledge of a dozen or more subjects into him, and coach him in five or six sporting disciplines. Instead of retiring at night to his own small suite of Palace rooms, he shared a dormitory with six other boys, and endured the occasional ribbing and somewhat less cosy routine that goes with public school life.

For all that, life was not so bad and there were the occasional moments of high excitement. Irish terrorism in the early 1970s led to Andrew's being protected day and night by Special Branch police officers (as was his cousin George, Earl of St Andrew's, who joined the school two years after he did). There was the famous incident of the school outing punch-up, when a group of Heatherdown boys in Andrew's school party were involved in a fight with other boys during a visit to the Natural History Museum in London. And there was the time in 1971 when Andrew became the school's first television star, after he had appeared with the Queen and Prince Edward, thumbing through the royal family album during the royal Christmas message.

Academically, Andrew proved no brighter that his elder brother, though his sporting abilities matched his tremendous enthusiasm for competitive games. Already a sound swimmer and keen sailor – by now he was a regular visitor to Cowes Week with his father – he ultimately represented his school in the senior rugby and cricket teams. It seemed to provide him with good enough credentials for Gordonstoun, and that was where he went in the Autumn of 1973.

Outgoing, extrovert, active and competitive, Andrew fitted the school's sensible new regime handsomely.

The Fergusons

The Fergusons are of Gaelic origin so, like Diana, Sarah brings Irish blood into the Royal Family. Like her, too, Sarah can claim royal blood, as both descend from Charles II: one of his mistresses is Diana's forebear; another, Lucy Walters, is Sarah's. Through her father's father Sarah is the Duke of Gloucester's cousin; another ancestor wed into the Lascelles family into which the Queen's aunt, the Princess Royal, married; and Sarah is also the Queen Mother's fifth cousin three times removed. She is also related to Sam Whitbread, the brewery founder, to Bess of Hardwick, a ruthless political opportunist of Tudor times, and to Mrs Fitzherbert, yet another royal mistress – George IV's. No doubt ancestral Ferguson ghosts rejoice that Sarah's liaison is royal *and* respectable!

Socially, he still had a lot to learn, the tendency towards arrogance which Heatherdown teachers had observed with concern some years earlier becoming as much a handicap as being trailed from pillar to post by his personal detectives or being fawned upon or snubbed by colleagues, depending upon what view they took of his royal status. And as time went on, he found that rarely could he form even the most innocent and platonic of attachments to members of the opposite sex – the thirty girls in the school in 1973 increased in number annually – without grossly inaccurate or exaggerated stories reaching the press.

Indeed it was at about this time that his fast-developing good looks and easy

manner with the girls began to earn him the reputation of a royal ladies' man. For several months there was serious speculation that he was already destined to marry Amanda Knatchbull, a granddaughter of Lord Mountbatten, who had joined the school at the same time as Andrew. It was not, considering Mountbatten's almost lifelong ambition to keep his family linked with the Windsors, a bad long shot but, like many subsequent tales of what was supposed to have gone on behind Gordonstoun's well-guarded doors, it proved well wide of the mark.

In a move similar to that taken with regard to Prince Charles, Andrew spent a couple of terms in 1977 abroad, in one of Gordonstoun's exchange arrangements. Whereas the elder brother had gone to Australia, the younger was sent to Canada for a six-month spell at Lakefield College in Ontario. The college's 'healthy mind, healthy body' motto found expression in vigorous physical opportunities, from cross-country ski-ing to kayaking, and in constant encouragement towards intellectual pursuits.

Always a doer rather than a spectator, and eager to try anything once, Andrew took to the college's ways like a duck to water. He joined its hockey team (and was 'suitably vicious when necessary'), continued with a pottery course he had started at Gordonstoun, proved himself 'really first class' on skis, joined a windsurfing group, and did some white water paddling on the Petawa river.

But here, as at Gordonstoun, it wasn't long before his interest in the country's female population – or possibly more correctly, their interest in him – took over. He had already, much to his embarrassment, found himself the focus of an hysterical reception from teenage girls on his very arrival in Toronto, but that was only the beginning. When he went skiing with a Lakefield pupil, Martha Anderson, she was in the eyes of the press as good as engaged to him. Andrew countered by arranging a reunion with Sandi Jones, who had been his companion during his previous year's visit to Montreal for the 1976 Olympics. He took her sailing, then to a reception, then to a jazz concert in Toronto, and finally to

(Below) the Royal Standard is the Queen's personal Standard, and is raised wherever she happens officially to be – whether in residence or on duty. Its 'quarterings' show the component parts of her United Kingdom of Great Britain and Northern Ireland – clockwise from top left, England, Scotland, Northern Ireland, Wales. Modifications of the Royal Standard are created when the Queen visits Commonwealth countries of which she is still Queen.

(Right) Westminster Abbey, which celebrated its 900th anniversary in 1965. It took almost 500 years to finish – completed by the addition of the twin towers in 1745.

The Palace and The Abbey

It is almost ten centuries since Edward the Confessor founded the present Westminster Abbey. Though he intended it as a monastery, his successor Harold was crowned there in 1066, and it has since become the sanctified coronation place for English and British sovereigns. Henry III rebuilt most of it in 1245, and decided that he would be buried there in a tomb next to the Confessor's. Subsequent kings (up to George II) copied his example, choosing the Abbey for a resting place, and Henry VII added a chapel where he and his wife, Elizabeth of York, were buried. Two of his grandchildren, Mary I and Elizabeth I, are also entombed in the Abbey along with a host of royal infants who lie in Innocents' Corner, and the mothers of Henry VII and James I. By happier tradition, Westminster Abbey has seen royal weddings with increasing regularity this century. One of Queen Victoria's youngest granddaughters, Princess Patricia of Connaught, was married there in 1919, and George V's only daughter, the Princess Royal followed suit in 1922. The future George VI married the present Queen Mother there in 1923, in a ceremony which she made memorable by placing her bouquet on the tomb of the Unknown Warrior. The Abbey tradition has been broken only three times since then. In 1935, the Duke of Gloucester's marriage to Lady Alice Montagu-Douglas-Scott (now Princess Alice), scheduled for the Abbey, was held in Buckingham Palace's Chapel Royal because of the recent death of the bride's father. The Duke of Kent's wedding in 1961 was held at York Minster, near his bride's family home. And, of course, Prince Charles and Lady Diana Spencer were married at St Paul's Cathedral.

a college dance, where he infuriated all the other girls there by dancing almost exclusively with her. Oblivious of their pique, he gave Sandi his college scarf and a badge to remember him by.

The recounting of such incidents added fuel to the fires of popular passions. Hordes of young, moon-struck girls hopped along the boundaries of cricket and rugby pitches, screaming for the sporting prince in his natty flannels or trim shorts, and half-swooned every time he flashed what one described as 'his toothy smile' at them. And when on one occasion he went to Pittsburgh to support his college hockey team, the attentions lavished on him by the local girls made him the arch-enemy, for the day at least, of their boyfriends.

Despite the occasional sour note – 'I do hope he brought his woollies,' jeered a newspaper columnist after Andrew had intended a joke about Canada's weather – he throughly enjoyed Canada. He found time to travel westwards and northwards, visiting the Pacific coast and the Arctic. He saw how the Eskimos build kayaks and prepare polar bear skins for tanning, visited three major wildlife parks, was proclaimed 'Heir of the Earth' by the Algonquin Indians, and hooked – then lost – his first salmon off Victoria. That the total experience was one he relished both at the time and as a memory, is proved by the fact that it brought him voluntarily back to Canada six years later.

In mid-1983, his former headmaster at Lakefield organised a great-outdoors expedition along the Nahanni River in the Northwest Territories' Mackenzie Mountains, and invited Andrew to join some twenty college students, former students and members of staff. He seized the opportunity with both hands, and for the best part of three weeks he canoed his way along fast-flowing rivers, shooting rapids, negotiating dangerous waterfalls, and paddling through canyons hundreds of metres deep for over two hundred miles. Added to that were miles of back-packing through wilderness and wild bear country, and in weather that was less than kind. One spell of torrential rain lasted for no less than three days, but it only drew out Andrew's sense of humour: dripping wet in green combat trousers, an old shirt, black Army boots and a

Different life styles: (left) Andrew with Senior Service shipmates; (above) Sarah leaving home for work.

shapeless, bottle-green camouflage hat, he said: 'I shall have to speak to mother about fixing this weather!'

'Not being first in line to the Throne,' wrote Rosalie Shann of the *Sunday Graphic* two days after Andrew was born, 'the Prince will obviously be able to choose his own career. And I wouldn't be in the least surprised if, within fifteen years from this date, we had another sailor Prince in the Royal Family. Imagine how delighted Prince Philip would be!' It was, of course, a pretty safe guess, even if the timing was four years out. But, true to form, the second son of the sovereign took to the Royal Navy once again. Early

in 1979, Andrew applied to join the Senior Service and was accepted in May of that year for a twelve-year short service commission as a helicopter pilot. In September he entered the Royal Naval

A day of celebration second only to his wedding: Andrew's triumphant Falklands return is greeted by the Queen.

Training College at Dartmouth for a four-month course, and comfortably passed his qualifying exams. He 'passed out' of Dartmouth in April 1980, and the Queen came to take the Salute at the passing-out parade and inspect the guard of honour of which he formed part. Needless to say, neither mother nor son could resist a brief smile as the Queen walked past.

It seems at first sight a contradiction that, having joined the Navy, Andrew should spend most of his career flying helicopters. It marks not only the way the Navy has changed since the days when it was associated wholly and solely with ships, but also Andrew's versatility and open-mindedness. While in his final years at Gordonstoun (which he left in 1979 with 'A' level passes in English, History and

Economics & Political Science), he had learned to fly gliders, had been awarded his parachutist's badge after a Royal Air Force course, and had been taught to fly to solo standard in a two-week course at RAF Benson. Now, his naval career pushed him further towards his goal of combining flight and sailing – of, as he once put it, 'living to fly, and to fly from the sea.'

Within a year of his passing out from Dartmouth, not only had he successfully completed a four-month flying training course in a Bulldog aircraft and his basic helicopter flying training at Culdrose in Cornwall, but he also took the prize for the best pilot on the course. Prince Philip was there to present him with his wings, and looked as delighted as the *Sunday Graphic's* prophet had foretold two decades earlier. It was then that his definitive career as a qualified and trained helicopter pilot began, though at the time he had little inkling of what 1982 was to bring.

In April of that year he was suddenly called off Easter leave, which he was spending at Windsor Castle, to join the general alert after the Argentinians had invaded the Falkland Islands. The prospect of his actually going to war prompted hasty consultations between the Ministry of Defence, the Prime Minister and the Queen, as to whether it was wise to send Andrew into possible battle, but the Queen was in no mood to prevaricate on this supreme question of duty. Nor was Andrew's commanding officer, who barked uncompromisingly, 'Prince Andrew is a serving officer and will do whatever is required of him. He's a member of my crew and flies like any other man. That's the way we play it.'

The Argentinians, already cock-a-hoop at having stolen a march on the British, derided Andrew's approach as his ship, HMS *Invincible* joined the Task Force from Portsmouth, announcing the imminent arrival of 'the Crown Prince of Colonialism' who 'should have brought

Though the celebration of a safe return, and its memory, lasted a long time, Andrew's first Cenotaph wreath bore a label in remembrance of British servicemen killed in the Falklands.

Task Force Log

Prince Andrew was called up from leave on 3rd April, 1982 and next day sailed with almost 1,000 colleagues on board the 19,500-ton aircraft carrier HMS *Invincible* from Portsmouth. *Invincible* arrived off the Falklands late that month. As a member of 820 Helicopter Squadron, Andrew's duties involved reconnaissance flying, seeking and rescuing survivors of naval encounters, and acting as decoy for enemy missiles. The Falklands were recaptured on 14th June, but *Invincible* and her crew stayed on until August, returning to Portsmouth on 17th September after 166 days' away. For his part in the conflict, Andrew was awarded the South Atlantic Medal, and has associated himself with the Falklands Appeal and the South Atlantic Fund in their attempts to alleviate physical and financial suffering among thousands of wounded soldiers and the dependent families of the 256 who died.

his nappies with him.' Meanwhile 'H', as Andrew was called, prepared for an onslaught that was not long in coming. At the end of April he was out rescuing a crewman from his sister ship *Hermes*, whose helicopter was lost; and was flying over the wreck of HMS *Sheffield*, the first major casualty of the conflict. The sight of wreckage and carnage, and smell of smoke and fumes are engraved on his memory to this day, and he swears he will never forget it.

From that point he was out on a round-the-clock duty involving reconnaissance, rescue, and acting as a decoy for the Exocet missiles of the sort that had destroyed *Sheffield*. Experiencing war at first hand, and being as vulnerable as anyone in the conflict that killed over 250 Britons, made him feel indefinably 'different'. I think my life has gone round the corner since I left for the Falklands. I felt lonely more than anything else. When you are down on the deck, when there are missiles flying around, then at that precise moment you are on your own and that's all there is. On the odd occasion I was terrified. To overcome fear I tried to adopt a positive mental attitude. I can't actually remember what I thought of – what I put in my mind – but I just remember telling myself, "I am going to survive this."'

Survive he did, as did *Invincible's* crew of almost a thousand souls. And when they came back to Britain after almost six months' absence, the Queen was there to greet them – and him. So were thousands of their relatives, encapsulating their collective relief and patriotism in banners like the one addressed to the Queen which announced: 'Well done, Mum; we're glad Andy's home.'

'Home' was a relative term. Andrew has, since then, and for one reason or another, been away from Britain almost as often as not. Naval duties have taken him to the Americas and the West Indies, holidays to the Caribbean and Canada, official duties to St Helena, Ascension Island, the United States and Canada again. He has hardly been in any one place long enough for anyone to speculate seriously about his getting spliced. Which is why, when he was spotted escorting Sarah Ferguson into

the Royal Enclosure at Ascot on that sunny June day in 1985, there was just a ripple of rumour – nothing more – that here might be the Queen's next daughter-in-law.

It was not until the turn of the year that the ripple became a wave. Sarah was invited to spend part of the Royal Family's New Year break with them at Sandringham. The press were stiffened into a sense of duty which never fails them at times like these, and they surrounded the private estate as if their lives depended on it. They were duly rewarded when, through long lenses, they distinguished Andrew and Sarah walking together so close that they could well have been holding hands – and that, for royalty, was enough to set the pulses racing.

The Diana syndrome took over from there. Sarah's Clapham home and the Mayfair office where she worked, the George Street sandwich bar where she used to have lunch, and the discos she frequented became obligatory waiting points for photographers and journalists alike. Predictably, there were no further clues in the hide-and-seek game until the truly unexpected occurred – and by royal instigation. In early February, Prince Charles and his family went to see Andrew on board his latest ship, HMS *Brazen*, then on a courtesy visit to the Pool of London. It was a private engagement as royal engagements go, but the rarity of seeing the whole Wales family out in public brought the press out in force. The unexpected bonus – Sarah in tow, even though ostensibly as Diana's companion – bestowed upon the press all the confirmation it could have asked for.

When the Prince and Princess of Wales

All smiles: (left) Andrew back in Portsmouth to open the Mountbatten Centre; and (above) acknowledging a huge cheer from the people of Newport, Rhode Island.

went to Klosters for a skiing holiday almost directly afterwards, and lined up for their customary photo-call with Sarah once again only metres away, there was the feeling that she was either the future Princess Andrew or the most shameless red herring Buckingham Palace had ever thrown the media's way. She was swamped by flashing cameras and shouted questions when she returned to London a few days later, and from then was given a police escort to and from work (which prompted one churl to ask whether this was because her life was in danger – or were the Metropolitan Police now providing a chaperone service?)

The Fergusons were at Charles' wedding – (left) Major Ronald is third row back, 11 seats to the right – which prompts the question: Who gets invited? Royal weddings being private affairs, the list should strictly be limited to family, friends, colleagues and acquaintances. As many of the Queen's relatives belong to other royal families, a sizeable European royal delegation is unavoidable. Many of her friends are from the aristocracy, so titles abound among the guests. Colleagues and acquaintances often include politicians, so parliamentarians of all parties have to be invited. Only then is there room for friends of bride and groom – Andrew's Navy colleagues, sporting companions, his household, and small social circle; and Sarah's closest colleagues from her working days, and a chosen band of Sloane Ranger friends.

They need not have worried on either count. No-one loves a lover more than the press, and Sarah seemed almost to be revelling in the publicity. Like Diana before her, she fielded all the usual questions with polite good humour and infuriating discretion. Once her car failed to start; another time she had difficulty getting out of a tight parking space; on other occasions she had to drive almost recklessly fast to lose her pursuers. Yet, without exception, she handled them all with tight-lipped, unprotesting confidence and aplomb.

'It has been quite an ordeal for a country girl,' said her father, when it was all over. 'I am extremely proud of her. She has behaved absolutely perfectly, never holding her head down, always being

'Everyone loves a story like this...' – and sent a telegram to the happy couple to say that the engagement 'would give great joy throughout the country.' Sarah's grandmother, Lady Elmhirst, said that the family was 'very happy indeed and very honoured. It's a nice fairy tale.'

Andrew's shipmates on *Brazen* received the news direct from the groom-to-be by telephone. By all accounts he sounded as bubbly as the champagne they broke open to celebrate, though it might have been otherwise had he realised that he had not closed his mess bill and his colleagues were counting on putting the cost of the celebration on it. Pupils at Daneshill School were allowed to watch the couple being interviewed on television. Staff at

advertisement appeared on behalf of the makers of Ferguson televisions. 'Trust a Ferguson to get a good reception at the Palace!' it trumpeted, adding proudly that their sets now came 'with something no other set can match – the bride's name on the front.'

Somehow, this seemed to say it all. Sarah was already a household name and would soon follow Diana into that world of transition from relatively unknown

(Below) Andrew escorting Princess Diana to Trooping the Colour. Now Sarah will sit beside him in those unique royal landaus – Britain's latest royal recruit, and fourth lady in the land.

polite, always smiling, yet never giving anything away.' His reaction, though he confessed himself 'reasonably emotional', was about the quietest of anybody's that day. Prince Charles said he could not be more delighted: 'I think she's wonderful... but then, I'm biased.' The Prime Minister oozed her delight –

Dummer's Queen public house concocted a lethal looking cocktail of champagne, orange juice and Monterez liqueur, called it Fergie's Fizz, sold it at £1.20 a glass – purple umbrellas and all – and it flowed like the Thames at high tide.

Meanwhile, the admen were ready and waiting. The following day a full-page

commoner to the wife of a prince of the blood royal. That means facing more than your fair share of publicity, good and bad, toeing a line you may not have realised existed before, and above all having to do as Andrew advised her as she first approached the cameras on that famous visit to HMS *Brazen* – 'Keep smiling!'